A New True Book

ZION

NATIONAL PARK

By David L. Petersen

 CHILDRENS PRESS®

CHICAGO

Erosion shaped many of the rock formations in Zion National Park

PHOTO CREDITS
UPI/Bettmann—35 (left and center)
© Reinhard Brucker—26, 28 (top and bottom left), 33
H. Armstrong Roberts—© J. Messerschmidt, 36; © George Hunter, 44; © D. Muench, 45
© Jerry Hennen—Cover
Historical Pictures/Stock Montage—35 (right)
PhotoEdit—© Jose Carillo, 28 (bottom right)
Photri—6
© Branson Reynolds—9 (2 photos), 12, 15, 16 (2 photos), 17 (top right and below right), 18 (left and right), 21, 25, 30, 37, 38, 42, 43
Root Resources—© Diana Stratton, 8, 19, 41; © James Blank, 10 (bottom); © Kitty Kohout, 18 (center)
Tom Stack & Associates—© Brian Parker, 14 (top); © Doug Sokell, 23
Tony Stone, Worldwide/Chicago—© John I. Ray, 2; © George Hunter, 24; © G. Brad Lewis, 39
SuperStock International, Inc.—© Tom Algire, 4
Valan—© Wayne Lankinen, 13 (left); © Esther Schmidt, 13 (right); © Robert C. Simpson, 14 (bottom); © Jeff Foott, 17 (center), 20 (right); © Don McPhee, 20 (left)
Horizon Graphics map—7
Cover—Zion Canyon from Angel's Landing

Project Editor: Fran Dyra
Design: Margrit Fiddle

Library of Congress Cataloging-in-Publication Data

Petersen, David.
   Zion National Park / by David Petersen.
     p.   cm. — (A New true book)
   Includes index.
   Summary: Describes the canyons, rock formations, plants, and wildlife found in Utah's Zion National Park.
   ISBN 0-516-01336-X
   1. Zion National Park (Utah)—Juvenile literature. 2. Natural history—Utah—Zion National Park—Juvenile literature. I. Title.
F832.Z8P48 1993
979.2'48—dc20   92-35048
                             CIP
                             AC

TABLE OF CONTENTS

A PARADISE

When people first came to what is now called Zion Canyon, about 1,500 years ago, they probably wanted to stay forever.

With its big trees, gurgling river, and strange rock formations, the canyon must have seemed like a paradise to the Native Americans.

The Mormon pioneers who came to the canyon hundreds of years later agreed with the Native Americans. The Mormons named this place *Zion,* which means "heavenly paradise."

Zion Canyon

6

ZION NATIONAL PARK

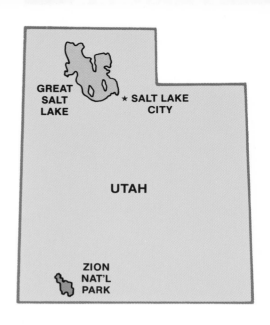

Zion National Park is in Utah. Elevations there range from 3,800 feet at the southern end, up to 9,000 feet in the north. Since the temperature falls as altitude increases, Zion has every climate from low, hot deserts to high, cool plateaus.

If you enter the park from

Checkerboard Mesa

the east, on the Zion-Mount Carmel Highway, you'll begin seeing strange shapes in the rocks right away.

Look for Checkerboard Mesa—a huge sandstone cliff that's cut into rectangles.

Hoodoos come in many different shapes and sizes.

It looks just like a giant checkerboard. You'll also see weird standing columns called "hoodoos."

Before reaching the canyon bottom, you'll pass through two tunnels cut

The Virgin River flows through Zion Canyon.

through solid rock. One of them is more than a mile long.

Finally, you enter Zion Canyon, with its red and white sandstone walls towering 2,000 to 3,000 feet above you.

The Virgin River flows through the canyon bottom. Along the river's bank grow grasses as high as a horse's belly. There are big trees and wildflowers of every color.

Ferns grow in Zion's hanging gardens.

In places, water drips from the cliffs, giving life to moisture-loving plants such as ferns, mosses, and wildflowers. These green spots on Zion's cliffs are called hanging gardens.

WILDLIFE AT ZION

Wildlife is everywhere. Most noticeable are the birds. Within the park, 271 kinds of birds have been identified.

The pine siskin (left) and Steller's jay (right) are found in Zion National Park.

Deer mouse (left) and mountain lion (above)

And you'll probably see some furry wildlife as well. Mammals such as deer, rabbits, and squirrels can be spotted in the campgrounds and along the park's miles of hiking trails. Zion is home to 72 kinds of mammals—from tiny mice to mountain lions.

Zion has several varieties of amphibians. These include salamanders, toads, and frogs. One of the most interesting of these is the canyon tree frog. It lives in and near water, but sometimes it climbs trees.

Tree frogs

The collared lizard (left) has black-and-white bands across its neck. The horned lizard (right) has large scales on its head that look like horns.

The park's reptiles include 14 kinds of lizards and 12 kinds of snakes. You'll see lots of the bold lizards, but not many of the shy snakes.

Zion is also a paradise for plant life. More than 800 species of plants live in Zion. Many of these are wildflowers.

A few wildflowers—such as golden columbines, scarlet monkey flowers, and lavender shooting stars—grow in the hanging gardens and other damp, cool places. But most—

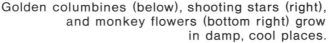

Golden columbines (below), shooting stars (right), and monkey flowers (bottom right) grow in damp, cool places.

Sacred datura (left), Indian paintbrush (center), and penstemon (right), are some of the many wildflowers that grow in the rocky park.

including Indian paintbrush, penstemon, and the sacred datura—thrive throughout the park.

Among Zion's trees, the giant cottonwoods are the most spectacular.

Cottonwoods need lots of water, so they grow near the river.

The high, sunny canyon slopes are the home of "pygmy forests" of squat

Cottonwood trees

Juniper tree (left) and quaking aspen (right)

pinyon pines and junipers.

And highest up, on the cool plateaus, grow white-barked quaking aspens, tall ponderosa pines, and slender fir trees.

Zion National Park is very much alive. And the green living heart of the park is Zion Canyon.

20

View of Zion Canyon from Scout's Lookout

Without the canyon and its river, there would be no colorful sandstone cliffs, no hanging gardens, no hoodoos, no Checkerboard Mesa, and no paradise for plants, wildlife, and people.

But how did such a deep, narrow canyon come to be?

21

HISTORY LESSON IN STONE

The rock in the walls of Zion Canyon was deposited as blowing desert sands back in the time of the dinosaurs. Gradually, the sand grains became cemented together to form sandstone.

For the last 13 million years, the gritty water of the Virgin River—like liquid sandpaper—has worn down through the sandstone of Zion, slowly carving Zion Canyon.

At the north end of Zion
Canyon is a place called
The Narrows. Here the river

Gateway to the Narrows

The Narrows gorge

has carved a "slot canyon" 2,000 feet deep and as narrow as 18 feet!

If you study the cliffs, you'll see lots of lines in the rock. These lines mark layers

of sandstone deposited at
different times.

Some layers lie flat. Others
were deposited unevenly as
sand dunes. In many places,
these flat and slanted layers

Sandstone cross-bedding

meet each other at odd angles. This is called "cross-bedding."

Cross-bedding, slot canyons, and checker-boarding are just three of the many fascinating natural wonders of Zion.

HUMANS AT ZION

The first people to visit
Zion about 1,500 years ago
were the Anasazi. *Anasazi* is
a Navajo word. It means "the
Ancient Ones."

When the Anasazi first
came to Zion, they camped
in caves or built shelters of
brush. They lived nomadic
lives, hunting and gathering
wild plants. They wove

Anasazi pottery (above). The Anasazi made sandals (below, left) from the tough leaves of the yucca plant (right).

baskets and sandals from
the tough fibers of the yucca
plant.

Later, the Anasazi settled
down to farm, build
permanent homes, and
make beautiful pottery.

The Anasazi left behind
many examples of their art.
Ancient engravings in rock
are called petroglyphs.
Paintings on rocks are called
pictographs. Examples of
Anasazi petroglyphs and

Anasazi petroglyphs carved on a canyon wall.

pictographs are hidden among Zion's canyons.

Then, about 800 years ago, the Ancient Ones disappeared from Zion. In fact, they deserted their entire Four Corners homeland—a large desert area surrounding the point where the states of Utah, Colorado, Arizona, and New Mexico touch corners.

Scientists believe a long drought forced the Anasazi out. Eventually, the Ancient Ones joined the Pueblo people of New Mexico and Arizona.

After the Anasazi were gone, the Southern Paiutes came to Zion. Like the early

Anasazi, the Paiutes hunted and gathered wild foods.

The Paiutes called the canyon *Mukuntuweap;* which means "place so narrow you must come out the same way you go in."

The Paiutes were still there in the mid-1800s, when the first white settlers arrived. The settlers wanted Zion Canyon and its water for farms and ranches. They forced the Native Americans out.

* mu • KOON • tu • weap

The Great White Throne

These newcomers were Mormons, a very religious people. They gave Zion its current name and bestowed religious names—like West Temple, Angel's Landing, and the Great White Throne— on many of its features.

In the early 1900s, the U.S. government purchased the big canyon from the Mormons so that it could be enjoyed by everyone.

In 1909, President Taft made the canyon into a protected area called Mukuntuweap National Monument.

In 1918, the monument was enlarged and its name was changed to Zion. In

Left: Herbert J. Grant, president of the Mormon Church, in 1920. Center: Stephen Mather, director of the National Park Service, and Walter Ruesch, superintendent of Zion National Park, at the dedication of the park. Right: President William Howard Taft.

1919, Congress made Zion a national park.

Finally, in 1956, Zion National Park was enlarged to its present size—229 square miles, or 147,000 acres.

Zion Canyon Scenic Drive

WHEN YOU VISIT ZION

Zion Lodge

What is there to do at Zion National Park? Most visitors enjoy the 13-mile Zion Canyon Scenic Drive. Stop and have lunch at the Grotto picnic area. Later, visit Zion Lodge for an ice cream cone.

Many people like to camp at one of the park's two riverside campgrounds. There they can swim, wade,

37

Visitors can explore the park on horseback.

ride bicycles, and explore.

There are horses for rent and ranger-guided nature walks, too.

But hikers have the most fun at Zion. A short trail

Weeping Rock

leads up to the big hanging garden called Weeping Rock. Its "tears" of dripping water feel great on a hot summer day.

From Weeping Rock, hikers can grab their canteens and head for the steep, mile-long hike up to Hidden Canyon. (This narrow slot canyon makes a great hideout.)

For a slightly longer hike, follow the loop trail to Emerald Pools. It's steep in places, but it's worth the climb to see the waterfall and the lovely canyon pools.

Hikers must be careful on trails with steep drop-offs. Some trails in

Lower
Emerald
Falls

Zion are not for people who have a fear of heights.

The most popular hike in Zion Canyon is Gateway to The Narrows Trail. It's an easy, scenic walk along the river in the narrow upper part of Zion Canyon.

Of course, one of your first stops in the park should be at the Zion Visitor Center. There you'll find museum displays explaining the geology, wildlife, and human history of Zion.

A model of Zion Canyon is on display at the Visitor Center.

Junior Rangers hike along a canyon trail.

And best of all, if you are 6 to 12 years old, you can join the Zion Junior Rangers.

Every Tuesday through Saturday during summer, Junior Ranger activities are held twice a day at the Zion Nature Center. If you

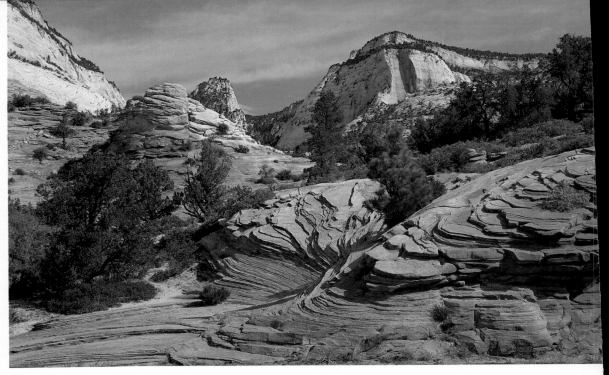

This petrified dune formation of Navajo sandstone
is called "Sandstone Symphony."

complete this program, you'll
earn an official Zion Junior
Ranger patch.

Zion National Park is truly
a paradise on Earth. Many
visitors, like those first
Anasazi people long ago,
never want to leave.

WORDS YOU SHOULD KNOW

altitude (AL • tih • tood) — the height of something above the earth's surface

amphibian (am • FIB • ee • yun) — an animal that lives both on land and in water

Anasazi (an • uh • SAH • zee) — the people who lived in the Four Corners area of the American Southwest until about seven hundred years ago

canyon (KAN • yun) — a long, narrow valley that has high cliffs on each side

cliff (KLIF) — a high, steep rock face that goes down sharply

columbine (KAH • lum • byne) — a wild plant that has colorful flowers with long spurs on the back

deposited (dih • PAH • zih • tid) — laid down or dropped by wind or running water

desert (DEH • zert) — a dry area that gets very little rainfall

drought (DROWT) — a lack of normal rainfall over a period of months or years

dune (DOON) — a hill of sand piled up by the wind

elevation (el • ih • VAY • shun) — height

engraving (en • GRAY • ving) — a work of art made by cutting into a hard surface

geology (gee • AH • luh • gee) — the study of the earth's features and history

hoodoo (HOO • doo) — a tall column of rock shaped by wind and water

juniper (JOO • nih • per) — a small evergreen tree that has dark blue-gray berries

mammal (MAM • il) — one of a group of warm-blooded animals that give birth to live young, have hair, and nurse their young with milk

mesa (MAY • sa) — a high, rocky hill having steep sides and a flat top

nomadic (no • MAD • ik) — moving from place to place to find food

Paiutes (PIE • yoots) — a group of Native Americans living in the western United States

paradise (PAIR • uh • dice) — a place that is very beautiful and that has all the things people need to live

penstemon (PEN • stih • mun) — a wild plant with showy, colorful flowers

permanent (PER • ma • nint) — lasting a long time

petroglyph (PEH • tro • glif) — a rock carving

pictograph (PIK • to • graf) — a painting on rock

pinyon (PIN • yun) — a kind of pine tree that has large seeds called pinyon nuts

plateau (plat • OH) — an area of elevated flat land

rectangle (REK • tang • gil) — a shape having four corners that is longer than it is wide

reptile (REP • tyle) — a cold-blooded animal with dry, scaly skin. It has a backbone and very short legs — or no legs at all

rock formations (RAHK for • MAY • shunz) — large rock shapes carved by wind or water

sacred datura (SAY • krid dah • TOO • ra) — a wild plant with long, trumpetlike flowers

salamander (SAL • uh • man • der) — a lizardlike animal that lives in or near water

sandstone (SAND • stoan) — a soft stone formed from sand that has been put under great pressure inside the earth

settlers (SET • lerz) — people who come to a new country and establish farms or other homes there

spectacular (spek • TACK • yoo • ler) — very showy; amazing

yucca (YUK • ah) — a tall plant with long, stiff leaves that grows in dry places

INDEX

About the Author

David Petersen is a teacher and widely published nature writer living in the Four Corners region of the American Southwest.

11:45

CONNETQUOT PUBLIC LIBRARY
760 Ocean Avenue
Bohemia, NY   11716
516-567-5079

Library Hours:

Monday - Friday	10:00 - 9:00
Saturday	10:00 - 6:00

GAYLORD